# What To Do When I Die

A practical survival guide

Jackie Charley

ASTUTE PUBLISHING, UK

Published by Astute Publishing, UK in 2016
First edition; First printing

Design and writing © 2016 Jackie Charley

www.jackiecharley.com

All rights reserved. No part of this book may be reproduced or transmitted in any form or by any means, including but not limited to information storage and retrieval systems, electronic, mechanical, photocopy, recording, etc. without written permission from the copyright holder.

ISBN: 978-0-9956232-1-7

*In loving memory of my mum*
who was always better organised than I have ever been!

A portion of all proceeds from the sale of this journal and it's companion book - *On Reflection* - will be donated to the Silver Line charity.

Silver Line is a FREE confidential helpline providing information, friendship and advice to older people, open 24 hours a day, every day of the year.

www.thesilverline.org.uk

# Contents

How to use this book .................................................................................. 1.

Finance ..................................................................................................... 3.

    Household Services ............................................................................ 5.

    Financial Products ............................................................................ 19.

    Pensions ............................................................................................ 37.

    Savings .............................................................................................. 41.

    Subscriptions .................................................................................... 49.

    Charitable Giving .............................................................................. 55.

Vehicles .................................................................................................. 61.

Property ................................................................................................. 69.

Household Practicalities ....................................................................... 73.

Pets ........................................................................................................ 77.

Untangling the Web .............................................................................. 85.

The Trick is ... ....................................................................................... 91.

Coming to a Close ................................................................................ 95.

Further Thoughts ................................................................................ 101.

Resources ........................................................................................... 105.

# How to use this book

The purpose of this book is to help **you** record what you know about running a home - with all its associated finance and responsibilities - because it may still be a complete mystery to your partner! It gives you the opportunity to capture that knowledge and store it in one memorable place ready to share.

Your family is really going to thank you!

Since no two couples run their household in the same way, some parts of this book may be more useful to you than others. You may want to add things that have not yet been included, or ignore some of those that have. That's fine - make it yours, and make it work for you!

The journal has been divided into the following chapters with easy-to-fill-in question and answer sections, plus blank pages for note-taking and adding extra thoughts:

- Finance
- Vehicles
- Property
- Household Practicalities
- Pets
- Untangling the Web (online accounts, memberships etc)
- The Trick is ... (your family's unique routines for solving unique problems!)
- Coming to a Close (discussion prompts with space to record end of life arrangements)
- Further Thoughts (space for additional musings, inspirations or questions to address)
- Resources

To get the most out of this book work through it with your partner. You'll be giving them the gift of your knowledge, and giving yourself peace of mind.

# Finance

The subject of finance covers a wide range of topics, some of which are quite complex in their own right. To help make this chapter more manageable it has been divided into the following sections:

- Household Services
- Financial Products
- Pensions
- Savings
- Subscriptions
- Charitable Giving

Pensions and Savings could have been included in the Financial Products section, but for ease of reference they have each been given a section of their own.

In addition, there are several untitled sections at the end of the chapter in which to include details of any financial arrangements which may not fit into these broad categories.

If you have a lot of financial investments it's likely that you will have a separate portfolio in which to hold their details. This section, however, will be of particular help to those of us who simply want to keep on top of our household's relatively modest expenditure and receipts.

# Household Services

Pages at the end of this section have been left blank for you to fill in other services unique to your household.

Service: Gas

Customer No. or Reference No. _____

Supplier: _____

Address: _____

Telephone: _____

Website: _____

Account paid from: _____

Approx amount: _____

Payment Terms:

☐ Weekly  ☐ Monthly  ☐ Quarterly  ☐ Annually

Payment Type:

☐ Direct Debit  ☐ Standing Order  ☐ Cash  ☐ Other

Payment Date: _____

# Household Services Cont'd

Service:  Electricity          Customer No. or  _____
                               Reference No.

Supplier: _____

Address:  _____
          _____
          _____
          _____

Telephone: _____   Website: _____

Account paid from: _____   Approx amount: _____

Payment Terms:

☐ Weekly    ☐ Monthly    ☐ Quarterly    ☐ Annually

Payment Type:

☐ Direct Debit    ☐ Standing Order    ☐ Cash    ☐ Other

Payment Date: _____

## Household Services Cont'd

Service:   Water

Supplier: _____

Address: _____

_____

_____

_____

Customer No. or _____
Reference No.

Telephone: _____    Website: _____

Account paid from: _____    Approx amount: _____

Payment Terms:

☐ Weekly    ☐ Monthly    ☐ Quarterly    ☐ Annually

Payment Type:

☐ Direct Debit    ☐ Standing Order    ☐ Cash    ☐ Other

Payment Date: _____

# Household Services Cont'd

Service: <u>Oil</u>　　　　　　　　Customer No. or Reference No. _____

Supplier: _____

Address: _____
_____
_____
_____

Telephone: _____　　　　Website: _____

Account paid from: _____　　　Approx amount: _____

Payment Terms:

☐ Weekly　　☐ Monthly　　☐ Quarterly　　☐ Annually

Payment Type:

☐ Direct Debit　　☐ Standing Order　　☐ Cash　　☐ Other

Payment Date: _____

# *Household Services Cont'd*

Service: __TV Licence__      Customer No. or
                             Reference No. _____

Supplier: _____

Address: _____

_____

_____

_____

Telephone: _____      Website: _____

Account paid from: _____      Approx amount: _____

Payment Terms:

☐ Weekly   ☐ Monthly   ☐ Quarterly   ☐ Annually

Payment Type:

☐ Direct Debit   ☐ Standing Order   ☐ Cash   ☐ Other

Payment Date: _____

## Household Services Cont'd

Service: Tel No: _____ Customer No. or _____
(landline) Reference No.

Supplier: _____

Address: _____
_____
_____
_____

Telephone: _____  Website: _____

Account paid from: _____  Approx amount: _____

Payment Terms:

☐ Weekly   ☐ Monthly   ☐ Quarterly   ☐ Annually

Payment Type:

☐ Direct Debit   ☐ Standing Order   ☐ Cash   ☐ Other

Payment Date: _____

# Household Services Cont'd

Service:    Tel No: _____      Customer No. or _____
             (mobile)                Reference No.

Supplier: _____

Address: _____

_____

_____

_____

Telephone: _____      Website: _____

Account paid from: _____      Approx amount: _____

Payment Terms:

☐ Weekly      ☐ Monthly      ☐ Quarterly      ☐ Annually

Payment Type:

☐ Direct Debit      ☐ Standing Order      ☐ Cash      ☐ Other

Payment Date: _____

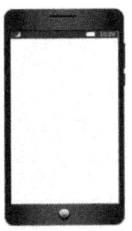

# Household Services Cont'd

Service: <u>Council Tax</u>　　　　Customer No. or _____
　　　　　　　　　　　　　　　　Reference No.

Supplier: _____

Address: _____

_____

_____

_____

Telephone: _____　Website: _____

Account
paid from: _____　Approx
　　　　　　　　　　　　　　　　amount: _____

Payment Terms:

☐ Weekly　　☐ Monthly　　☐ Quarterly　　☐ Annually

Payment Type:

☐ Direct Debit　☐ Standing Order　☐ Cash　　☐ Other

Payment
Date: _____

# Household Services Cont'd

Service: _____     Customer No. or _____
                                   Reference No.

Supplier: _____

Address: _____

_____

_____

_____

Telephone: _____     Website: _____

Account paid from: _____     Approx amount: _____

Payment Terms:

☐ Weekly     ☐ Monthly     ☐ Quarterly     ☐ Annually

Payment Type:

☐ Direct Debit     ☐ Standing Order     ☐ Cash     ☐ Other

Payment Date: _____

## Household Services Cont'd

Service: _____  Customer No. or _____
                                 Reference No.

Supplier: _____

Address: _____
         _____
         _____
         _____

Telephone: _____  Website: _____

Account paid from: _____  Approx amount: _____

Payment Terms:

☐ Weekly     ☐ Monthly     ☐ Quarterly     ☐ Annually

Payment Type:

☐ Direct Debit   ☐ Standing Order   ☐ Cash   ☐ Other

Payment Date: _____

## Household Services Cont'd

Service: _____        Customer No. or _____
                                Reference No.

Supplier: _____

Address: _____
_____
_____
_____

Telephone: _____        Website: _____

Account paid from: _____        Approx amount: _____

Payment Terms:

☐ Weekly        ☐ Monthly        ☐ Quarterly        ☐ Annually

Payment Type:

☐ Direct Debit    ☐ Standing Order    ☐ Cash    ☐ Other

Payment Date: _____

# Household Services Cont'd

Service: _____   Customer No. or _____
                                 Reference No.

Supplier: _____

Address: _____

_____

_____

Telephone: _____   Website: _____

Account paid from: _____   Approx amount: _____

Payment Terms:

☐ Weekly   ☐ Monthly   ☐ Quarterly   ☐ Annually

Payment Type:

☐ Direct Debit   ☐ Standing Order   ☐ Cash   ☐ Other

Payment Date: _____

*Household Services Cont'd*

Service: _____   Customer No. or _____
                                 Reference No.
Supplier:
         _____

Address:
         _____

         _____

         _____

         _____

Telephone: _____   Website: _____

Account
paid from: _____   Approx
                                    amount: _____

Payment Terms:

☐ Weekly     ☐ Monthly     ☐ Quarterly     ☐ Annually

Payment Type:

☐ Direct Debit   ☐ Standing Order   ☐ Cash   ☐ Other

Payment
Date: _____

In the following section complete all those that apply and/or include new entries of your own.

# Financial Products

Product: Mortgage

Customer No. or
Reference No. _____

Lender: _____

Address: _____

_____

_____

_____

Telephone: _____

Website: _____

Account paid from: _____

Approx amount: _____

Payment Terms:

☐ Weekly  ☐ Monthly  ☐ Quarterly  ☐ Annually

Payment Type:

☐ Direct Debit  ☐ Standing Order  ☐ Cash  ☐ Other

Payment Date: _____

# *Financial Products Cont'd*

Product:   Rent

Landlord: _____

Address: _____

_____

_____

_____

Customer No. or
Reference No. _____

Telephone: _____

Website: _____

Account paid from: _____

Approx amount: _____

Payment Terms:

☐ Weekly    ☐ Monthly    ☐ Quarterly    ☐ Annually

Payment Type:

☐ Direct Debit    ☐ Standing Order    ☐ Cash    ☐ Other

Payment Date: _____

# *Financial Products Cont'd*

Product:   Loan                    Customer No. or
                                   Reference No. _____
Company   _____

Address:  _____

          _____

          _____

          _____


Telephone: _____           Website: _____

Account                             Approx
paid from: _____           amount: _____

Payment Terms:

☐ Weekly        ☐ Monthly        ☐ Quarterly        ☐ Annually

Payment Type:

☐ Direct Debit  ☐ Standing Order  ☐ Cash             ☐ Other

Payment
Date: _____

# Financial Products Cont'd

Product: House Insurance

Customer No. or Reference No. _____

Company

Address: _____

Telephone: _____

Website: _____

Account paid from: _____

Approx amount: _____

Payment Terms:

☐ Weekly  ☐ Monthly  ☐ Quarterly  ☐ Annually

Payment Type:

☐ Direct Debit  ☐ Standing Order  ☐ Cash  ☐ Other

Payment Date: _____

## *Financial Products Cont'd*

Product: Life Insurance        Customer No. or
                               Reference No. _____
Company
Address: _____

_____

_____

_____

Telephone: _____   Website: _____

Account
paid from: _____   Approx
                                    amount: _____

Payment Terms:

☐ Weekly     ☐ Monthly     ☐ Quarterly     ☐ Annually

Payment Type:

☐ Direct Debit   ☐ Standing Order   ☐ Cash   ☐ Other

Payment
Date: _____

# *Financial Products Cont'd*

Product: Medical Insurance

Customer No. or Reference No. _____

Company: 

Address: _____
_____
_____
_____

Telephone: _____

Website: _____

Account paid from: _____

Approx amount: _____

Payment Terms:

☐ Weekly ☐ Monthly ☐ Quarterly ☐ Annually

Payment Type:

☐ Direct Debit ☐ Standing Order ☐ Cash ☐ Other

Payment Date: _____

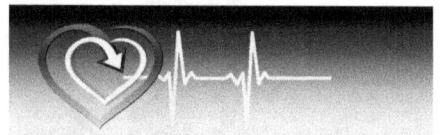

## *Financial Products Cont'd*

Product: <u>Credit Card</u>　　　　Customer No. or
　　　　　　　　　　　　　　　　Reference No. _____

Company: _____

Address: _____

_____

_____

_____

Telephone: _____　　　Website: _____

Account paid from: _____　　　Approx amount: _____

Payment Terms:

☐ Weekly　　☐ Monthly　　☐ Quarterly　　☐ Annually

Payment Type:

☐ Direct Debit　　☐ Standing Order　　☐ Cash　　☐ Other

Payment Date: _____

---

Please note: There is no space on this page to record your card number or other sensitive details. These should be stored securely elsewhere. See the section on passwords for further information.

# Financial Products Cont'd

Product: Credit Card

Customer No. or Reference No. _____

Company:

Address: _____
_____
_____
_____

Telephone: _____

Website: _____

Account paid from: _____

Approx amount: _____

Payment Terms:

☐ Weekly  ☐ Monthly  ☐ Quarterly  ☐ Annually

Payment Type:

☐ Direct Debit  ☐ Standing Order  ☐ Cash  ☐ Other

Payment Date: _____

# *Financial Products Cont'd*

Product: <u>Credit Card</u>　　　Customer No. or Reference No. _____

Company: _____

Address: _____

Telephone: _____　　　Website: _____

Account paid from: _____　　　Approx amount: _____

Payment Terms:

☐ Weekly　　☐ Monthly　　☐ Quarterly　　☐ Annually

Payment Type:

☐ Direct Debit　　☐ Standing Order　　☐ Cash　　☐ Other

Payment Date: _____

# Financial Products Cont'd

Product: Store/Loyalty Card       Customer No. or
Store: _____            Reference No. _____

Address: _____
_____
_____
_____

Telephone: _____        Website: _____

Account paid from: _____    Approx amount: _____

Payment Terms:

☐ Weekly    ☐ Monthly    ☐ Quarterly    ☐ Annually

Payment Type:

☐ Direct Debit   ☐ Standing Order   ☐ Cash   ☐ Other

Payment Date: _____

## *Financial Products Cont'd*

Product: Store/Loyalty Card                Customer No. or
Store:                                     Reference No. _____

Address: _____

_____

_____

_____

Telephone: _____          Website: _____

Account                                   Approx
paid from: _____          amount: _____

Payment Terms:

☐ Weekly          ☐ Monthly          ☐ Quarterly          ☐ Annually

Payment Type:

☐ Direct Debit    ☐ Standing Order   ☐ Cash               ☐ Other

Payment
Date: _____

# Financial Products Cont'd

Product: Store/Loyalty Card                   Customer No. or
Store:                                        Reference No. _____

Address: _____
         _____
         _____
         _____

Telephone: _____           Website: _____

Account
paid from: _____           Approx
                                     amount: _____

Payment Terms:

☐ Weekly    ☐ Monthly    ☐ Quarterly    ☐ Annually

Payment Type:

☐ Direct Debit    ☐ Standing Order    ☐ Cash    ☐ Other

Payment
Date: _____

*Financial Products Cont'd*

Product: <u>Store/Loyalty Card</u>　　　Customer No. or
Store:　　　　　　　　　　　　　　　Reference No. _____

Address: _____

_____

_____

_____

Telephone: _____　　　Website: _____

Account paid from: _____　　Approx amount: _____

Payment Terms:

☐ Weekly　　☐ Monthly　　☐ Quarterly　　☐ Annually

Payment Type:

☐ Direct Debit　☐ Standing Order　☐ Cash　　☐ Other

Payment Date: _____

30

# *Financial Products Cont'd*

Product: Payment Plan      Customer No. or Reference No. _____

Provider:

Address: _____
_____
_____
_____

Telephone: _____     Website: _____

Account paid from: _____     Approx amount: _____

Payment Terms:

☐ Weekly     ☐ Monthly     ☐ Quarterly     ☐ Annually

Payment Type:

☐ Direct Debit     ☐ Standing Order     ☐ Cash     ☐ Other

Payment Date: _____

Reason for this payment plan: _____
_____
_____

# Financial Products Cont'd

Product: <u>Payment Plan</u>　　　　Customer No. or
　　　　　　　　　　　　　　　　Reference No. _____

Provider:

Address: _____

_____

_____

_____

Telephone: _____　Website: _____

Account paid from: _____　Approx amount: _____

Payment Terms:

☐ Weekly　　☐ Monthly　　☐ Quarterly　　☐ Annually

Payment Type:

☐ Direct Debit　☐ Standing Order　☐ Cash　　☐ Other

Payment Date: _____

Reason for this payment plan: _____

_____

_____

# Notes

# Notes

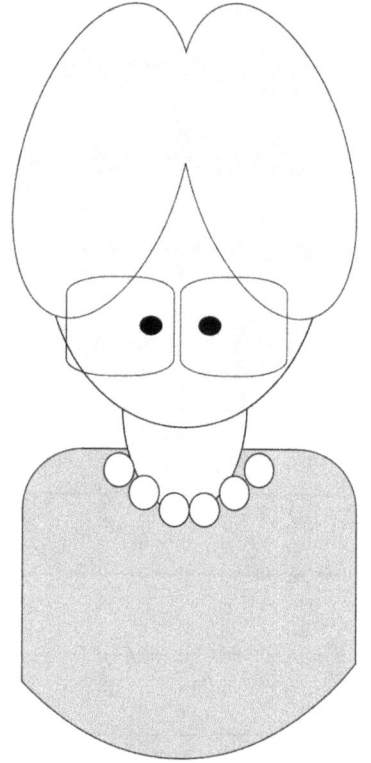

# Pensions

Pension Provider: _____

Tel: _____  Ref: _____

Are you still contributing to this pension? Yes ☐  No ☐

Have details of an alternative beneficiary Yes ☐  No ☐
been lodged with the Provider?

If you have already started drawing on    Yes ☐  No ☐
this pension can the remaining funds be
transferred to an alternative
beneficiary?


Pension Provider: _____

Tel: _____  Ref: _____

Are you still contributing to this pension? Yes ☐  No ☐

Have details of an alternative beneficiary Yes ☐  No ☐
been lodged with the Provider?

If you have already started drawing on    Yes ☐  No ☐
this pension can the remaining funds be
transferred to an alternative
beneficiary?

*Pensions Cont'd*

Pension Provider: _____

Tel: _____          Ref: _____

Are you still contributing to this pension? Yes ☐   No ☐

Have details of an alternative beneficiary Yes ☐   No ☐
been lodged with the Provider?

If you have already started drawing on      Yes ☐   No ☐
this pension can the remaining funds be
transferred to an alternative
beneficiary?


Pension Provider: _____

Tel: _____          Ref: _____

Are you still contributing to this pension? Yes ☐   No ☐

Have details of an alternative beneficiary Yes ☐   No ☐
been lodged with the Provider?

If you have already started drawing on      Yes ☐   No ☐
this pension can the remaining funds be
transferred to an alternative
beneficiary?

# Notes

# Notes

# Savings

*Guard well within yourself that treasure, kindness.
Know how to give without hesitation, how to lose without regret, how to acquire without meanness.*

*John Wanamaker*

# *Savings Cont'd*

Product: _____     Account No. _____

Account
Name: _____

Bank: _____

Address: _____

_____

_____

_____

Telephone: _____     Website: _____

Account
paid from: _____     Amount
per payment: _____

Payment Terms:

☐ Weekly   ☐ Monthly   ☐ Quarterly   ☐ Annually

Payment Type:

☐ Direct Debit   ☐ Standing Order   ☐ Cash   ☐ Other

Payment
Date: _____

# Savings Cont'd

Product: _____   Account No. _____

Account Name: _____

Bank: _____

Address: _____
_____
_____
_____

Telephone: _____   Website: _____

Account paid from: _____   Amount per payment: _____

Payment Terms:

☐ Weekly    ☐ Monthly    ☐ Quarterly    ☐ Annually

Payment Type:

☐ Direct Debit    ☐ Standing Order    ☐ Cash    ☐ Other

Payment Date: _____

## *Savings Cont'd*

Product: _____     Account No. _____

Account
Name: _____

Bank: _____

Address: _____
_____
_____
_____

Telephone: _____     Website: _____

Account
paid from: _____     Amount
per payment: _____

Payment Terms:

☐ Weekly     ☐ Monthly     ☐ Quarterly     ☐ Annually

Payment Type:

☐ Direct Debit     ☐ Standing Order     ☐ Cash     ☐ Other

Payment
Date: _____

*Savings Cont'd*

Product: _____     Account No. _____

Account
Name: _____

Bank: _____

Address: _____

Telephone: _____     Website: _____

Account
paid from: _____     Amount
per payment: _____

Payment Terms:

☐ Weekly     ☐ Monthly     ☐ Quarterly     ☐ Annually

Payment Type:

☐ Direct Debit     ☐ Standing Order     ☐ Cash     ☐ Other

Payment
Date: _____

# Notes

# Notes

This section deals with smaller, regular payments to organisations that could include:

- Magazines
- Motoring Associations
- Professional Bodies
- Online membership sites
- Hobby groups
- Gym memberships
- Others

It also offers a prompt to help you decide whether you want to cancel the subscription or continue with it.

# Subscriptions

Name of Publisher/Group/Association/Club: _____

Type: _____
Eg. Membership, Magazine, etc.

Reference No: _____
(If known)

Contact: _____

Telephone: _____

Amount: _____

Account paid from: _____

Cancel?  Yes ☐  No ☐

---

Name of Publisher/Group/Association/Club: _____

Type: _____
Eg. Membership, Magazine, etc.

Reference No: _____
(If known)

Contact: _____

Telephone: _____

Amount: _____

Account paid from: _____

Cancel?  Yes ☐  No ☐

# Subscriptions Cont'd

Name of
Publisher/Group/Association/Club: _____

Type: _____     Reference No: _____
Eg. Membership, Magazine, etc.    (If known)

Contact: _____     Telephone: _____

Amount: _____      Account
                                paid from: _____

Cancel?     Yes ☐    No ☐


Name of
Publisher/Group/Association/Club: _____

Type: _____     Reference No: _____
Eg. Membership,                   (If known)
Magazine, etc.

Contact: _____     Telephone: _____

Amount: _____      Account
                                paid from: _____

Cancel?     Yes ☐    No ☐

## Subscriptions Cont'd

Name of
Publisher/Group/Association/Club: _____

Type: _____     Reference No: _____
Eg. Membership, Magazine, etc.     (If known)

Contact: _____   Telephone: _____

Amount: _____    Account
                                  paid from: _____

Cancel?     Yes ☐     No ☐


Name of
Publisher/Group/Association/Club: _____

Type: _____     Reference No: _____
Eg. Membership,                   (If known)
Magazine, etc.

Contact: _____   Telephone: _____

Amount: _____    Account
                                  paid from: _____

Cancel?     Yes ☐     No ☐

## Subscriptions Cont'd

Name of
Publisher/Group/Association/Club: _____

Type: _____          Reference No: _____
Eg. Membership, Magazine, etc.   (If known)

Contact: _____        Telephone: _____

Amount: _____         Account
                                  paid from: _____

Cancel?     Yes ☐     No ☐


Name of
Publisher/Group/Association/Club: _____

Type: _____          Reference No: _____
Eg. Membership,                  (If known)
Magazine, etc.

Contact: _____        Telephone: _____

Amount: _____         Account
                                  paid from: _____

Cancel?     Yes ☐     No ☐

*Subscriptions Cont'd*

Name of
Publisher/Group/Association/Club: _____

Type: _____        Reference No: _____
Eg. Membership, Magazine, etc.      (If known)

Contact: _____        Telephone: _____

Amount: _____        Account
                                    paid from: _____

Cancel?        Yes ☐      No ☐


Name of
Publisher/Group/Association/Club: _____

Type: _____        Reference No: _____
Eg. Membership,                     (If known)
Magazine, etc.

Contact: _____        Telephone: _____

Amount: _____        Account
                                    paid from: _____

Cancel?        Yes ☐      No ☐

# Charitable Giving

Which charities do you currently support? Would you like to continue supporting them or not?

Name of Organisation: _____

Purpose: _____

Tel: _____     Website: _____

Amount: _____     Account paid from: _____

Payment Terms:

☐ Weekly       ☐ Monthly       ☐ Quarterly       ☐ Annually

Continue to support?     Yes ☐     No ☐

# Charitable Giving Cont'd

Name of Organisation: _____

Purpose: _____

Tel: _____    Website: _____

Amount: _____    Account paid from: _____

Payment Terms:

☐ Weekly    ☐ Monthly    ☐ Quarterly    ☐ Annually

Continue to support?    Yes ☐    No ☐


Name of Organisation: _____

Purpose: _____

Tel: _____    Website: _____

Amount: _____    Account paid from: _____

Payment Terms:

☐ Weekly    ☐ Monthly    ☐ Quarterly    ☐ Annually

Continue to support?    Yes ☐    No ☐

# Charitable Giving Cont'd

Name of Organisation: _____

Purpose: _____

Tel: _____  Website: _____

Amount: _____  Account paid from: _____

Payment Terms:

☐ Weekly   ☐ Monthly   ☐ Quarterly   ☐ Annually

Continue to support?   Yes ☐   No ☐

Name of Organisation: _____

Purpose: _____

Tel: _____  Website: _____

Amount: _____  Account paid from: _____

Payment Terms:

☐ Weekly   ☐ Monthly   ☐ Quarterly   ☐ Annually

Continue to support?   Yes ☐   No ☐

# Charitable Giving Cont'd

Name of Organisation: _____

Purpose: _____

Tel: _____  Website: _____

Amount: _____  Account paid from: _____

Payment Terms:

☐ Weekly   ☐ Monthly   ☐ Quarterly   ☐ Annually

Continue to support?   Yes ☐   No ☐


Name of Organisation: _____

Purpose: _____

Tel: _____  Website: _____

Amount: _____  Account paid from: _____

Payment Terms:

☐ Weekly   ☐ Monthly   ☐ Quarterly   ☐ Annually

Continue to support?   Yes ☐   No ☐

# Charitable Giving Cont'd

Name of Organisation: _____

Purpose: _____

Tel: _____  Website: _____

Amount: _____  Account paid from: _____

Payment Terms:

☐ Weekly  ☐ Monthly  ☐ Quarterly  ☐ Annually

Continue to support?  Yes ☐   No ☐

Name of Organisation: _____

Purpose: _____

Tel: _____  Website: _____

Amount: _____  Account paid from: _____

Payment Terms:

☐ Weekly  ☐ Monthly  ☐ Quarterly  ☐ Annually

Continue to support?  Yes ☐   No ☐

# Vehicles

Remember, this section concerns all and any vehicle for which you have responsibility - cars, motorbikes, spaceships - the lot!

**Registration No:** _____
(License Plate)

**Make:** _____  **Model:** _____

Insurance Co: _____

Telephone: _____  Contact: _____

Payment due: _____

Do I want to keep this vehicle?   Yes ☐   No ☐

If no, ask the insurance company if I can get a refund when the vehicle is no longer required.

Does it have breakdown cover?   Yes ☐   No ☐

With whom? _____  Tel: _____

Normal garage used: _____  Tel: _____

MOT due: _____  Tax due: _____

When tax is due, ask if I can get a refund if vehicle is no longer needed.

# Vehicles Cont'd

**Registration No:** _____
(License Plate)

**Make:** _____ **Model:** _____

Insurance Co: _____

Telephone: _____ Contact: _____

Payment due: _____

Do I want to keep this vehicle?    Yes ☐    No ☐

If no, ask the insurance company if I can get a refund when the vehicle is no longer required.

Does it have breakdown cover?    Yes ☐    No ☐

With whom? _____ Tel: _____

Normal garage used: _____ Tel: _____

MOT due: _____ _____

When due, ask if I can get a refund if vehicle is no longer needed.

# Vehicles Cont'd

**Registration No:** _____
(License Plate)

**Make:** _____ **Model:** _____

Insurance Co: _____

Telephone: _____ Contact: _____

Payment due: _____

Do I want to keep this vehicle?   Yes ☐   No ☐

If no, ask the insurance company if I can get a refund when the vehicle is no longer required.

Does it have breakdown cover?   Yes ☐   No ☐

With whom? _____ Tel: _____

Normal garage used: _____ Tel: _____

MOT due: _____ _____

When due, ask if I can get a refund if vehicle is no longer needed.

*Vehicles Cont'd*

**Registration No:** _____
(License Plate)

**Make:** _____  **Model:** _____

Insurance Co:   _____

Telephone:   _____ Contact: _____

Payment due:   _____

Do I want to keep this vehicle?   Yes ☐   No ☐

If no, ask the insurance company if I can get a refund when the vehicle is no longer required.

Does it have breakdown cover?   Yes ☐   No ☐

With whom?   _____ Tel: _____

Normal garage used:   _____ Tel: _____

MOT due:   _____ Tax due: _____

When due, ask if I can get a refund if vehicle is no longer needed.

# Vehicles Cont'd

**Registration No:** _____
(License Plate)

**Make:** _____    **Model:** _____

Insurance Co: _____

Telephone: _____    Contact: _____

Payment due: _____

Do I want to keep this vehicle?    Yes ☐    No ☐

If no, ask the insurance company if I can get a refund when the vehicle is no longer required.

Does it have breakdown cover?    Yes ☐    No ☐

With whom? _____    Tel: _____

Normal garage used: _____    Tel: _____

MOT due: _____    Tax due: _____

When due, ask if I can get a refund if vehicle is no longer needed.

# Notes

# Notes

# Property

Mortgage and rent payments are dealt with in the Finance section.

These pages are for recording the names and numbers of people you use on a regular basis to help maintain your home, or those you might need to contact in an emergency.

**Landlord**

Name: _____  Tel: _____

**Plumber**

Name: _____  Tel: _____

**Electrician**

Name: _____  Tel: _____

**Roofer**

Name: _____  Tel: _____

*Property Cont'd*

**Builder**
Name: _____   Tel: _____

**Gardener**
Name: _____   Tel: _____

**Window Cleaner**
Name: _____   Tel: _____

**Local Council**
Name: _____   Tel: _____


Name: _____   Tel: _____


Name: _____   Tel: _____

# *Property Cont'd*

Name: _____   Tel: _____

Name: _____   Tel: _____

Name: _____   Tel: _____

Name: _____   Tel: _____

Name: _____   Tel: _____

Name: _____   Tel: _____

# Property Cont'd

Name: _____  Tel: _____

Name: _____  Tel: _____

Name: _____  Tel: _____

Name: _____  Tel: _____

Name: _____  Tel: _____

Name: _____  Tel: _____

# Household Practicalities

This section is for all those niggly things that "someone" is supposed to know, but has often forgotten.

Bin collection days: _____

School holiday dates: _____

Where is the:

- Fuse box _____
- Electric meter _____
- Gas meter _____
- Water stopcock _____
- _____
- _____
- _____

# Notes

# Notes

# Pets

Ah! You think you know them...

After all, you feed them often enough, kick them off the sofa regularly, and unplug them from the vacuum cleaner at least once a week. Oh no, wait ... that was just their hair.

But would you know what type of food to buy, when to worm them, dose them or get them jabbed at the vet's if your partner wasn't there to do it?

You will now:

Vet
Practice: _____ Tel: _____

Address: _____
_____
_____
_____

*Pets Cont'd*

**Pet's name:** _____

**Feeding routine:**

Type of food: _____

_____ (approx amount) _____ times per day

**Medical routine:**

Tick and flea applications every _____ weeks

Vaccinations every _____ weeks/months

Worm every _____ weeks/months

Other _____

**Exercise routine:**

_____

**Other things to note:**

_____

_____

_____

_____

*Pets Cont'd*

**Pet's name:** _____

**Feeding routine:**

Type of food: _____

_____ (approx amount)  _____ times per day

**Medical routine:**

Tick and flea applications every _____ weeks

Vaccinations every _____ weeks/months

Worm every _____ weeks/months

Other _____

**Exercise routine:**
_____

**Other things to note:**
_____
_____
_____
_____

*Pets Cont'd*

**Pet's name:** _____

**Feeding routine:**

Type of food: _____

_____ (approx amount) _____ times per day

**Medical routine:**

Tick and flea applications every _____ weeks

Vaccinations every _____ weeks/months

Worm every _____ weeks/months

Other _____

**Exercise routine:**
_____

**Other things to note:**

_____

_____

_____

_____

*Pets Cont'd*

**Pet's name:** _____

**Feeding routine:**

Type of food: _____

_____ (approx amount)    _____ times per day

**Medical routine:**

Tick and flea applications every _____ weeks

Vaccinations every _____ weeks/months

Worm every _____ weeks/months

Other _____

**Exercise routine:**
_____

**Other things to note:**

_____

_____

_____

_____

*Pets Cont'd*

**Pet's
name:** _____

**Feeding routine:**

Type of
food: _____

_____ (approx amount) _____ times per day

**Medical routine:**

Tick and flea applications every _____ weeks

Vaccinations every _____ weeks/months

Worm every _____ weeks/months

Other _____

**Exercise routine:**
_____

**Other things to note:**

_____

_____

_____

_____

*Pets Cont'd*

**Pet's name:** _____

**Feeding routine:**

Type of food: _____

_____ (approx amount)   _____ times per day

**Medical routine:**

Tick and flea applications every _____ weeks

Vaccinations every _____ weeks/months

Worm every _____ weeks/months

Other _____

**Exercise routine:**
_____

**Other things to note:**

_____
_____
_____
_____

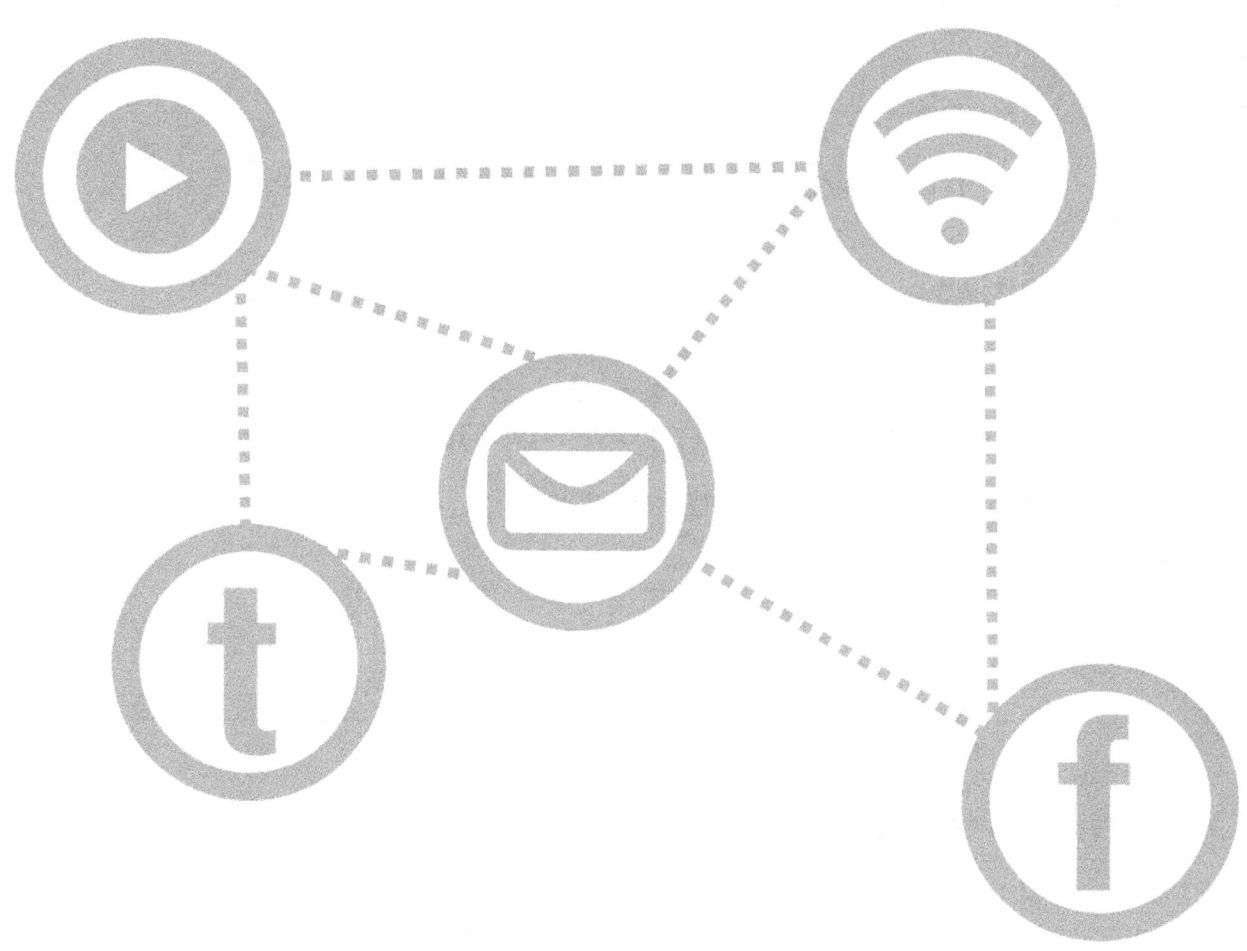

# Untangling the Web

This section gives you the opportunity to note down any online accounts that need to be closed, as well as taking a look at what to do with passwords.

**Passwords**

Oh joy! We love 'em, we hate 'em. But we definitely need to remember them.

Or do we?

Well no, actually.

We just need somewhere to store them and then remember where that "somewhere" is.

But it's not here! It's not in your purse, or the front of your diary. It's not in the back pocket of your jeans or tucked behind the car's sun visor.

One of the best ways to securely store your passwords is by using a password manager program. This holds them in a virtual online vault, and you simply have to remember the one password that opens the vault. Remembering one is definitely better than chasing the thirty-odd escapees running round your desk on bits of tattered paper.

If this is new to you, try one of these: 1Password, LastPass or Dashlane. (The last two are free.) For further information see the link to a helpful blog post in the Resources Section at the end of the book.

# Untangling the Web Cont'd

## Social Media

| | Do you need to close the account? | |
|---|---|---|
| Facebook | Yes ☐ | No ☐ |
| Instagram | Yes ☐ | No ☐ |
| YouTube | Yes ☐ | No ☐ |
| Twitter | Yes ☐ | No ☐ |
| LinkedIn | Yes ☐ | No ☐ |
| Other: ........................................ | Yes ☐ | No ☐ |
| Other: ........................................ | Yes ☐ | No ☐ |

## Trade Accounts

| | | |
|---|---|---|
| Name: ........................................ | Yes ☐ | No ☐ |
| Name: ........................................ | Yes ☐ | No ☐ |
| Name: ........................................ | Yes ☐ | No ☐ |

# *Untangling the Web Cont'd*

## Online Shopping Accounts

Name: ..........................................  Yes ☐  No ☐

Name: ..........................................  Yes ☐  No ☐

Name: ..........................................  Yes ☐  No ☐

Name: ..........................................  Yes ☐  No ☐

Name: ..........................................  Yes ☐  No ☐

Name: ..........................................  Yes ☐  No ☐

# Notes

# Notes

# The trick is...

This section is for recording those unique routines your partner does which carry a little magic or mystery for you, like how to keep their favourite plant alive despite all attempts to kill it. Or, how many times you have to pull the lawn mower cord before it finally kicks into life.

We've all got those little nuggets of know-how that make our lives run a little more smoothly.

This is where you put 'em.

The trick to _____

is _____

_____

_____


The trick to _____

is _____

_____

_____

*The Trick is... Cont'd*

The trick to _____

is _____

_____

_____


The trick to _____

is _____

_____

_____


The trick to _____

is _____

_____

_____

*The Trick Is... Cont'd*

The trick to _____

is _____

_____

_____


The trick to _____

is _____

_____

_____


The trick to _____

is _____

_____

_____

*Saying goodbye doesn't mean anything.*
*It's the time we spent together that matters, not how we left it.*

*Trey Parker*

# Coming To a Close

There are lots of very helpful sources which provide details on what must be done, both legally and practically, when a loved one dies.

Some of these are listed in the Resources section at the end.

However, these few pages provide important discussion points for you to talk about together before your life comes to a close.

It's so much better to leave clear instructions about these end-of-life issues to ensure that your family says "goodbye" in the way you would wish.

*Coming To a Close Cont'd*

## A Will

Have you made one?   Yes ☐   No ☐

Where is it? _____

Solicitor's name and address:

_____
_____
_____
_____
_____

Tel: _____

Does it need updating?   Yes ☐   No ☐

Have you considered organ donation?   Yes ☐   No ☐

Have you discussed it with your family?   Yes ☐   No ☐

Thoughts:

_____
_____
_____

# *Coming To a Close Cont'd*

## Funeral Arrangements

1. Do you know what you want?
   Here are just a few options to get you thinking:
   - Traditional Burial
   - Cremation
   - Natural Burial (shroud or biodegradable casket)
   - Woodland Burial
   - Living Funeral (see below)

2. Have you discussed your thoughts with family or friends?

3. Are there funds set aside for this?

4. Have you made a list of items you would like incorporated into your funeral service? For example, certains songs, poems, readings or speeches?

   Make a note of those you're beginning to consider here:

   _____

   _____

   _____

   _____

   _____

   _____

# Coming To a Close Cont'd

More ideas about things to include in your funeral service:

_____
_____
_____
_____
_____
_____
_____
_____
_____
_____
_____
_____
_____

*Coming To a Close Cont'd*

## A Living Funeral

It might sound strange to think of attending your own 'Living Funeral', but what better time to celebrate your life than while you're still here living it!

In fact, why not call it a 'Celebration of Life'?

Invite your friends and family just like you would to any other important occasion. Choose your own music and have a blast. Ask people to share their memories and say all the wonderful things they usually leave until it's too late for you to hear.

You could have something as intimate as a simple afternoon tea, or as lavish as a banquet - whatever's your style - but make it the party of a lifetime!

If you would like to explore ways of capturing your own significant memories of the people and places that have meant the most to you, you might like the companion journal to this book called *On Reflection: A Twilight Years Journal.*

*On Reflection...* is not meant to be an autobiography but a collection of meaningful reflections. There's plenty of room to be honest (about yourself or others), room to celebrate, and room to wonder. But above all, the opportunity to savour your life and pass its many treasures on to others. (See end of book for more details.)

# Further Thoughts...

This space is for you to jot down any further thoughts, questions, inspirations or concerns you have.

_____
_____
_____
_____
_____
_____
_____
_____
_____

*Further Thoughts Cont'd*

*Further Thoughts Cont'd*

*Further Thoughts Cont'd*

# Resources

## Advice

A wealth of advice and free resources concerning your preparation for, and what to do after someone dies, is provided by Dying Matters. Visit them at www.dyingmatters.org.

## Alternative Funerals

There is no legal requirement in the UK to use a funeral director. The Natural Death Centre provide help and advice on alternative funerals such as woodland burials, or family-led arrangements.

Visit: www.naturaldeath.org.uk.

## Benefits

The Bereavement Service is a telephone service that lets you:

- End a benefit claim for someone who has died
- Find out if you are eligible for benefits because your husband, wife or civil partner has died
- Make a claim for bereavement benefits or a claim for help with funeral costs, known as a Funeral Payment

Tel: 0345 606 0265 or visit the website at:
www.gov.uk/bereavement-payment

*Resources Cont'd*

### Living Funerals

For more inspiration on Living Funerals read this wonderful blog post at http://blog.cremationsolutions.com/living-funerals-the-party-of-a-lifetime/2016/01/

### Local Registry Office

Find your local registry office at www.gov.uk/register-offices

### Passwords

http://www.lifehack.org/articles/featured/10-free-ways-to-track-all-your-passwords.html

### Tell Us Once

Tell Us Once is a service that lets you report a death to most government organisations in one go. It operates in most parts of the UK, and your local registrar will be able to tell you if the service is available in your area.

For more details visit: www.gov.uk/after-a-death/organisations-you-need-to-contact-and-tell-us-once or just type "Tell Us Once" into your internet search engine.

### What To Do When Someone Dies Checklist

Find it at: www.nidirect.gov.uk/articles/what-do-when-someone-dies-checklist

*Resources Cont'd*

## Other Resources

Use this space to make notes and record other useful organisations you have come across.

_____
_____
_____
_____
_____
_____
_____
_____
_____
_____
_____
_____
_____

## Resources Cont'd

## Other Resources

Use this space to make notes and record other useful organisations you have come across.

# Notes

# Notes

# Notes

# About the Author

Jackie Charley is a writer and freelance editor who lives with her husband and two sons in the lovely Scottish Borders, along with two lively dogs and a gaggle of crazy chickens.

Before she began her editing career she worked as a Parent Coach and published a best-selling book, *'Unlock the Cage: Empowering Parents to Step out of Fear into Freedom'*.

She is currently working on a series of journals that aim to help people capture their moments of inspiration or expertise.

Here are a few of the things that fire up her days:

- "I love language, and I love people - being an editor is a brilliant way of combining the two. I get really excited by the way we communicate through language in all its weird forms – the smiles and nods, the grunts and gestures (you can tell I have teenage kids), our cultural symbols and, of course, the written word.

- I love witnessing someone's joy when they achieve a goal.

- I love ideas that make me think, and even re-think my viewpoint.

- I get energized by music, especially singing, because it's a great stress-buster and a wonderful way to make friends."

For more books by this author see overleaf.

# ALSO BY JACKIE CHARLEY

Look for more Journals in the 'Slice of Life' series coming soon!

*On Reflection: A Twilight Years Journal* is the companion book to this journal.

It will help you capture your most significant memories and store them all in one safe place.

The book is laid out with prompts to help you recall the people and places that have meant so much to you throughout your life. It also provides spaces for you to include photographs, sketches or favourite quotations under headings such as:

- Significant people in my life
- Places I've visited
- Books that have made the biggest impact on me
- Things I always wanted to say but never did...
- And much much more!

*On Reflection...* is not meant to be an autobiography, but a collection of meaningful reflections. There's plenty of room to be honest (about yourself or others), room to celebrate, and room to wonder. But above all, the opportunity to savour your life and pass its many treasures on to others.

Available on Amazon or from your local bookstore

ISBN: 978-0-9956232-0-0